THE VOICE OF LISTENING

BY 'A COMPILER'

RED BALLOON
PUBLISHING

COPYRIGHT

The Voice of Listening

Created with Vellum

THE VOICE OF LISTENING

This book is a product,

Garnered And Refashioned From Other
Sundry Sources

'GARFOSS'

A compiler's reflections on numerous dialogues at an ever-open global table.

CONTENTS

INTRODUCTION

After conversations in any of numerous situations, we all tend to recall our own contributions and to be a bit unsure about those of others. Yet an observer, knowing the participants and having won their trust in each exchange, might well hear strands of the unusual, even shafts of wisdom scattered in the to and fro of talk, that if blended would bring us all nearer to the integrity of this strange life in which we each and all are inextricably immersed. Thus, the title 'The Voice of Listening'.

The moderator of a wide variety of such open conversations, many of them in tiny gaps in situations of daily work, sought to be a trusted independent friend with an ear for any strands of the unusual and/or shafts of wisdom on living our complex lives. He evolved a process of reflection after such exchanges, which he expressed in broken text or rough-hewn verse, hoping to catch and share the value in an often-confusing world, the value of humbly learning from each other, as a small but vital step towards understanding and pursuing the Common Good. This moderator's role was termed 'Chaplaincy' but could be applied to any 'servant leadership', to a 'genuine enabler', to a 'trusted friend', or even to 'a stranger with an unexpected sensitivity and genuine attention to others'. By attributing these many pages of probing for the richness of our shared humanity to 'A Product of GARFOSS – *Garnered And Refashioned From Other Sundry Sources*', it is hoped we can together hit upon new ways of exploring the profound mantra 'Nothing is Impossible if you don't mind who gets the credit.'. A sentence that has lit up many minds when heard for the first time. It is the hope in these times, when the intertwining of Scientific and Spiritual consciousness is revealing more of the depth and range in each Discipline's search, that such broken verse would become a natural tool in our urgent deepening of the meaning and the achieving of a universal Common Good. That Common Good is the outcome of the eternal wisdom nestling in the interrelated terms of gift, 'God' and 'Gaia'.

THE WAY INTO 'THE VOICE OF LISTENING'

Troubled by slick answers to complicated and distorted questions on issues of 'faith' - that is, anyone's sense of human origin, life and purpose - and distressed by bright young people being put down by older workers grown cynical, I started asking questions on how to compare views of 'faith' in any dialogue that I could join or initiate. Thus, from a steel works; a coal-mine; a university sectioned ironically into academic boundaries; in the Christian Council for Monetary Justice; at coffee after worship; at an ever-open global online table, the exercise of aligning shafts of wisdom began.

The following pages of broken text flowed in as evolving surges and shafts from such dialogues, for consideration one by one, but also in their accumulated impression of our quest for global sanity and our own faithful participation in its restoration. They are clustered under four section heads:

1. Gaia and God-given context - CONTEXTUAL

2. Wisdom garnered from listening - 'GARFOSS'

3. Holistic, immersive and cosmic - FAITH SPECIFICS

4. Crises of the 2020s - RESTRUCTURING

SECTION 1

GAIA AND GOD-GIVEN CONTEXT

CONTEXTUAL

'Reflections spent on a year's senior management course'
PERSONAL ASPIRATIONS & POSITIONAL ARROGANCE

I must confess, we are as yet
so far from cosmic consciousness;
despite so many visions set in
mindful charters, declarations,
constitutions, statements of intent;
yet we still cannot beget, re-birth,
a state of common good and purpose,
maturity in coherence, prior unity.

We compromise those dreams
which from genesis in stardust and sunshine,
through growth in love and labour,
ages and ageing, thrusts of forward looking life,
we mistakenly resist the drag of bio-gravity,
submitting to the pull of individuation, so that
divisions and labels, that our love should heal,
defeat our best intentions.

Through profound relationship,
humanity as all natural phenomena,
conceives rich blending of all our
genderful cells, the DNA
of countless generations,

exciting the fast flow of new life
to maturing as another stage in
consciousness and reflection
the gift bestowed on species 'humanity.'

In this, our generation, the greatest cry
to mature responsibility, is for eternal wisdom,
common sense, ceaseless energy of procreation,
intended commitment to co-operation
summoning us to a maturing life, yes,
through inevitable individual deaths
to the grace of cosmic consciousness
our permanent bequest to future generations.

Exercising **Ego**-morality excites creative team-work,
stretching our **Ecu**-morality to consciously reflect
the **Eco**-morality of shared intent to honour nature.
Thus sensitivities of intimacy combine
in corporate complexity to form that global
consciousness
which transcends positional arrogance, the drive
and drag
of institutions, to thus reawaken personal aspirations
feeding cosmic consciousness for planetary survival.

'Humanity's 11th hour on earth looms'
WHY TRUSTEES ALL?

History is our hope. Earth's replenishment our intent.
The world is our responsibility.
We tell the story each with our own lives speaking what has gone before, is now and is to come.

We are responsive to all that has been,
response-able for what will be.
Responding, we construct new justice in our time.
We are a people not commissioned to preserve,
but to remember, to rebuild; not held in rigidity, but faithfulness.
We are a living legacy of human wholeness
rooted in the grasp of the divine.

Journeyer, is not now the time to travel,
to stand heart to heart as once others stood within a bend of time?
I will begin to speak and listen to you,
'cor ad cor loquitor', reaching always
for the best in both of us.
For it is within our sacred dreams,
our lifted vision of ourselves in endless creativity, that rests the journey home.
I am a citizen of this sacred planet.
today I walk the pilgrim ways again,
in my generation with you and all others,

reliving past earth-moments.
Clasped in the fervor of covenantal trust,
re-membering our covenantal gift
to nourish searching persons then and yet to come, to sanctify time,
humanity and earth, by nature's call, TRUSTEES ALL,
averting just in time, in the urgency of now, some horrendous species-ending fall.

In debt to Ann Johnson and various groups exploring stewardship.

‘Towards a solution’
I DREAMT I HEARD...

Of modern man found almost everywhere,
His heart transplanted by an ‘exploitation app’,
‘A fast accruing, surplus calculator’.

It led rapidly to hardening of his heart;
Almost beyond recovery. But he lingers,
Enticing others as his final fling.

He’s trying to fix things as they are
Trapped in exponential rapaciousness
Of the earth entire; a nightmare of destruction.

Our planet’s ecologically rich communities,
Have now all almost lost their hearts.
Don’t let us linger in that nightmare.

Let your true heart beat again,
Stirring once more our incarnational potential
To serve the Common Good within your range.

By carefully acting out the ‘Kin[G]dom of God.
Now move on to design and construct
new aspects of the Common Good
in our GAIAN zone of Cosmic location...

Group discussion on God and Gaia after the death of James Lovelock 7/22.

'Exploration and exponential growth are encultured by imperialism'

WHERE LIES THE FORCE OF NATURE

Not just the intellectual giants, nor inspired poets.
Not just great scholars, or instant-response quizzers.
Not those who stand out in a crowd of specialists.
Not master builders, gold medal athletes or tennis stars.

Every person, every creature, every blade of grass,
each ant, mountain, ocean, seed or thunderous storm,
flourishes by dint of nature's energy in ceaseless flow.
Accepting this will enhance our ability to help earth grow.

Rebecca Solnit pithily explains, 'Hope is not a lottery ticket',
but 'an axe you break down doors with in an emergency'.
'To hope is to give yourself knowingly to the future,
a commitment to make the present world inhabitable.'

'Hope in the Dark' is the call for the big structural change
we need in this survival emergency before us now.
Contribute to the urgent need of reparations and a just transition
to a world where all are fully human stewards of God's free gifts.

The pandemic has served well the clique of billionaires,
the world's 10 richest own more 'wealth' than
the world's poorest 40 percent of all humanity.
Current economic structures can hold no future place.

The key areas of pandemic profiteering are
such basic human necessities as food,
medicine, energy, technology and 'hope in the light'.
'So be it' depends on you and me playing our part.

On the run-in to a conference on 'Hope in the Dark' - July 2022.

'Behind a Basic Icon'
A SUMMING UP OF
HUMANITY IN NATURE

A SIMPLE ICON for the **PROFOUND MYSTERIES** of:

- **UBUNTU** - I am because we are

- **HUMANISM WITHIN A MYSTERY** - behind all faiths

- **INCARNATION** - cosmic energy in each of us

- **CO-EVOLUTION** – co-creative transformation.

- **UBIQUITOUS PRESENCE OF CREATIVE ENERGY**

- **SACRED LIFE WITHIN A SACRED PLANET**

- **COVENANTAL HUMAN TRUSTEESHIP**

An ICON as one image of many responses to the discussion of our human place in nature's endless flow.

'Value the Cosmic Matrix'
WOMB OF INTRINSIC VALUE - ECSTATIC WITH INTENT

Ecstatic, holding perspective,
Generously and inclusively conserving,
no position or label to defend exclusively,
every presentation to explore,
insights to evoke and share,
motivated by intrinsic value
in service of the common good
and the earth entire.

Not ownership or status, not self-justification,
not contract compliance, nor in conforming loyalty,
alert in crucial solidarity, yet always truth seeking,
where truth is no human truth oft hidden,
never fully revealed, often rediscovered,
vibrantly pertinent and applied to real economy;
inclusive, debt, dis-enslaving.

Interest only as true cost charging,
profiteering exacerbating poverty,
respectful of commitment, open to critique,
free for all, derogatory of none,
all alike enabled in response.
Value the womb, the matrix, flexible sac of creativity,
A mini-Gaian organism: true life on earth.

From a group discussing conception in human life.

'A 3-fold GAIAN perspective informing dialogue'
COHESION

We are required to value all our
intimate (*self-scape*),
corporate (*social-scape*), and
global (*earth-scape*)
observations, settings and experiences, between which
we needs must oscillate (*poietic-scape*).
This leads to my call that we need to nurture
a psyche the size of the earth (*Gaian identity)*,
(*tight coupling with the environment*),
within which to discover our own ecologically humble,
economically response-able, self.
This provides the imperative for inclusive justice
arriving only with public money free of debt and
interest,
and with property acquisition permissible
only when contributing to the common good.

Discussing Self-scape, Social-scape & Earth-scape by Poietic-scape.

'All matter originates and exists by virtue of a conscious and intelligent mind'
WONDERFUL. WE SHOULD HAVE HAD THEM FIRST or THINKING LIKE A GRANDFATHER

To hear one say, 'I'm not tired, I've just run out of imagination',
and another 'Go away, you're annoying my sleeping'.
Or later, disturbed when staring at the light,
'Colours have come out of the ceiling and are now in your eyes',
transforming to a 'Sunrise of wonder', a grandparent's delight.

No moralising, no talk of improving our mind,
just offering us an innocent enquiry by inspired spontaneity,
crossing forbidding boundaries to open up things
forgotten, and unseen or even undreamt, hard work made simple,
by these quintessential children's works of art.

'Fragility is a mark of value, that which is not fragile is pretentious',
so, tender children, still immune to rigid habits of adulthood,
come fresh to all the world. Safeguard such miracles.

'Sorry, I was daydreaming' said Grandfather, accused'.
'I call that not listening' retorts the sharp 4 year old.
Then 'Sophia's World' opens before us, we see,
astounded,
the gradual build-up of private discoveries,
bringing fresh vision, new hope,
and elders learning anew from our young
just how easy it is to unify the inner and the outer
worlds,
the ordinariness and the extraordinariness of
everything.'

The innocence or un-woundedness excites our adult curiosity.

'Our need to be tentative with words'
'I AND THOU' REVISITED IN LIFE AND DEATH'

Oneself, one's body, dies; the name begins to fade;
the hallmarks, benchmarks, dates, memories, vaguely
remain.
The inheritance of all our selves has been lived with,
expanded by a measure, then passed on.
Thus, this honoured heritage sends vital tributaries
to the ever swelling stream of life **itself.**

Not reification, but celebration, bold proclamation.
Each self is thus renewed, and not thereby excluded,
in purpose greater than ourselves; **itself** the greater
good.

Love, the infinite compassion, takes everyone's interest
seriously,
accurately estimates and supplies each other's needs,
unquestioningly accepts all excretions, and so becomes
oneself,
dying and yet risen, in quiet creative anonymity
in true self-effacement, before **the unseen face of God.**
All matter originates and exists only by virtue of a force
which brings the particles of an atom to vibration,
holding this most minute solar system of the atom
together.

We must assume behind this force the existence conscious and intelligent mind. **This mind is the matrix of all matter.'**

From an Open Global Table discussion excited by Resurgence - Autumn 2009.

'Our need to be tentative with words'

WONDER ABOUT YOUR WORDS

Worth in words lies with the recipient,
not the nagging ego of the author.
Words express intrinsic value of thoughts,
perchance for random readers or listeners;
evoking genuine dialogue, suppressing monologues,
not enhancing of the composer's self-esteem.
Copyright is a conceit controlling ownership
for we have no natural right to our Creator's gift.
Neutrality towards the gift of elocution
enriches the worth of words, increasing
the greater likelihood of dialogue, avoiding
a preacher's controlling charm, or professional's conceit.
No words are neutral, owned or controlled.
Every spoken, written, imagined utterance is for
the potential value to hearer, reader, casual listener:
not for the credit of the author, tempted to conceit.
Seek startling juxtaposition, surprising accentuation,
sudden exception to habitual or encultured
experiences.
Use your words humbly and tentatively,
searching consciously or unconsciously for common
ground among neighbours, each needing to extend the
common good.
Every word-smith's forge should determine
conversations with careful angles of surprise,
a longing for better understanding despite great odds.

In such pithy explorations in broken verse our phrases don't have attribution. Each offering is tested for authentic wisdom, before any conditioned response to a name detracts from weighing the impact.

‘Thoughts gathered at the ever open global table’
THE JOBBING KIN[G]DOM BUILDER IN US ALL

Never impossible - only - not yet achieved.
Within our future sense and integral intelligence,
all is present, flowing, incalculable potential,
‘I am’, in me, becoming all I might be;
You, astonished, reaching beyond your grasp;
We, inspired, transcending our conditioning;
rare hope formulating ordinarily,
as pragmatic purposes
are born again of universal principles.

Thus, rising cosmic consciousness,
enthused by moral imagination,
frames today's preparation
and each hour's ensuing act.
Wondering prayerfulness supersedes
mere mindfulness.
Promise, purpose, potential, when
all realised, restore the replenishing of earth.
The covenant of everything under the rainbow
thrives as multi-featured love in inclusive health:
thus reigns the Common Good.

Nothing is impossible
if you don't mind who gets the credit.
We are the Earth.
Cosmic creativity deserves both
the initial and the final credit, as we sense
the flowing symbiosis:
that is you and me absorbed and yet distinct
in one humanity.

We are the universe
reaching to understand itself.
Life in maturity is an evolutionary gift;
each composted life will one day nourish
seeds of distinguishable future forms.

You, a 'Kin[G]dom builder', are adding humbly
to an inclusive, non-hierarchical,
non-imperial humanity,
in your service to the healing
and maturing of this sacred planet.

Many discussions on the Kin[G]dom of God – Kin in the Ground of all Being.

'All life is Intimate, Social and Global'
NOT IN A HOLLOW NUTSHELL, JUST IN A GRAIN OF SAND

Online each day from myriad sources.
Expressions or exposures flow.
Exemplifying Blake's pithy aphorism;
'To see a world in a grain of sand,
and a heaven in a wildflower.
To hold Infinity in the palm of your hand,
and eternity in an hour.'
It is encouraging to hear how many are
Exploring, pursuing and populating that pithy wit.
The grain of sand cradles a Quantum alert,
While wild flowers flourish, permeating borders,
As Mystics and Indigenous people worldwide
Were long aware. We've little time to catch up.
Let's all determine to inspire, instil, elaborate,
Tackling political, economic, climate, ecological
emergencies.
In 'Citizens Juries' and deliberative democracy
Transforming our homes and local communities,
How we travel, all the daily work we do.
We must all work to end
THE THREEFOLD STRUCTURAL FAULT
Entrapping western societal governance,
Gripped by USURY, THEFT OF THE COMMONS,
And the CORPORATE INSTITUTIONAL DRAG,
Making task differentiation a belittling

POWER OVER OTHERS instead of
CO-OPERATIVE SHARING
OF APPROPRIATE SKILLS AND TASKS.

Caring for the natural world within our range
Is everyone's responsibility in setting
A clear example in healing people
through acts of justice and inclusion,
Embodying compassionate and nonviolent ways.
We must offer our vital, humble help to translate
Mystic Blake's beautiful quantum metaphor.

Insights garnered online and refashioned. No attribution is necessary.

'Through Cosmos and Gaia to Eternity'
NATURE > NURTURE > MATURITY > ETERNITY

The relentless flow of creativity,
from Nature, through Nurture, by Maturity, into Eternity,
is the activity some term God, or equivalent name 'I Am'.
We all have this stream of nascent energy in our being.
It is Global, Societal and Personal;
Universal, International, and Communal;
so quantum flow, by incarnation,
energises spirit as matter:
expressed by each human being 'in Christ',
when contributing to the Kin[G]Dom,
'Kin-ship' in the ' Ground of all Being';
with Jesus as a unique exemplar
in both passing history and lasting metaphor.
'GOD' is constant context; 'COMMUNITY' the human pretext;
but 'NOW' is the only text by which we live.

UBUNTU – A Coda

'I am because We are' - LIFE IN A SINGLE WORD.
Six simple letters, melded, grasped and dwelt upon consistently,
reveal the mysterious secret of the human quest for meaningful purpose.
So too the indivisible plea to love God and every neighbour.
Only thereby can each and all experience life's true self.

Evolving of Christian terminology, as a universal perception of stewardship.

'7 aspects of love explored at the global open table'
COME TO THE COMMON TABLE ATOP ITS GAIAN LEGS

Leg 1. Prior Unity, fundamental symbol of original creativity.
Leg 2. Ubuntu, 'we are' to overcome rampant individualism.
Leg 3. Recognised Wonders of ensuing infinite diversity.
Leg 4. Engagement mutually in pearls of wisdom shared.

There, seated side by side in a round of equal dignity,
seek humbly to compare all uses of language,
seek diligently to fortify the Common Good.
Be alms-ed, yes alms-ed, with generously gifted insights,
on freely fair sharing earth's life-ensuring gifted wealth.
Express ideas briefly for serious consideration.
Weigh with open mind both clear or stumbling responses.
Seek positive creative tension where differences,
often creatively apposite, are seen as rigid rivalries, as opposites.
requiring someone's victory and another's ignominious defeat.

Decorate the legs or polish the table if you wish to use
this exploration. It needs no attribution.
Yours in shared trusteeship of this sacred planet.

Love is ......

Eros: Life-generating sexual tenderness

Philia: Deep friendship of the will reaching our neighbours

Ludus: Light, tentative attention to life's idiosyncrasies

Agape: Fostering and nurturing community as communion

Pragma: Showing encompassing & enduring attention to others

Philautia: Realising our self-enhanced capacity to love God's entire creation

In online conversation with Extinction Rebellion - XR

'Action for a Universal Solution'
BOLDLY TO BEHOLD
[before digging deeper into change]

Decide simply to 'Behold', finding awe and wonder
everywhere.
Be present to what is,
free of the filter of preferences
or falsely measuring by 'importance'.

'Behold' opens up a broader, deeper,
wider field of perception, as
we find fresh ways of knowing, enjoying.
Yes, sensing whole-heartedly
that 'the soul is not in the body,
the body is in the soul'
where 'deep calls unto deep',
and love becomes ubiquitous.

Then coming back to Gaia, our mother Earth,
a new perspective flowering in mind,
we switch from soul to soil with fervour,
knowing 'Soil just might save us,
but we are going to have to save it first.'
Our very own nature has universal roots
that we must seek to cultivate cooperatively.

Online discussion on being out of our depth.

'Through the cosmic lens diversity unites us'
DIVERSITY IN PRIOR UNITY PROTECTED

Our collective human shadow
Deepens, darkens remorselessly,
Materialism, classism, racism, genderism,
All intermingling on many planes.

'Conversion', 'Metanoia', 'Nomos' vital
To a paradigm shift of dramatic scale,
A meta-narrative of relationships,
To be imagined and retained in vision.

Such a rich perception of equal dignity
For all planetary life, all peoples,
Ever emergent in each heart and mind,
Is necessary too in all supportive systems.

If privileged, dismantle your supremacy.
If struggling, claim your dignity and role.
Become mature in service of all life,
For every distinction includes all others.

Diversity is enhanced in prior unity,
With togetherness and difference both revered,
Beyond vital tribal nurturing and self-identity,
Into mature living out all right relationships.

Then humble science and true religion
Cohere in earth's eco-management, mirroring
creativity flowing ever on in life's attractiveness
and allurement. Thus UBUNTU.

From group recognition of Spirit/Energy animated, that is, incarnate. Such the wisdom in both Quantum Science and Mystic Faith.

'Crumbling foundations demand the choices of natural sensitivity'

GOLD, GREEN AND DOUBLE COMMITMENT

To contribute to the Kin[G]dom of God, practise **THE GREEN RULE** - do unto the Earth as you would have nature do unto you

THE GOLDEN RULE - do unto others as you would they do unto you

THE DOUBLE COMMITMENT binding them together as:
'Love both God and all neighbourly relationships in cosmic creativity.'

There's a psychic charge pulsating in society today,
a critical reminder that there's something unresolved.

And so the image of crumbling foundations must
persist,
indicative of the need for examining
'THE GAIA ATLAS OF PLANET MANAGEMENT',
providing its comprehensive challenge re the integrity
of all perspectives found in ancient Mystic sensitivities,
as in modern Quantum Physics
and the resultant expansion of
COSMIC CONSCIOUSNESS
as genuine Curative vision,
the indispensable context for
Palliative pragmatism.

A dialogue on how extensive the change must be and to widen our own response.

'Listening requires mind, ear, eye, and heart in harmony'

COLLABORATION NOT CATASTROPHE

From one prong of our network's extensive
thought and online penning, comes this wrestling
with how to replace the exploitative economy,
now hurtling humanity towards insanity

Faults, fallacies, false faux pas hidden in our words
form formidable barriers to sympathy or empathy,
and thence with any certainty to collaboration,
that vital element of loving God and neighbour
as integral part of our so-called selves

So journeying deeper into conversation,
reconcile each yes from you and no from me,
that we may be intelligible neighbours to each other,
regardless of distance, colour, status, skills
or terminology of both daily and specialised ways.

Let your prophetic imagination and pastoral sensitivity
inform the fashioning of every dialogue,
whether twixt friend or seeming enemy.

Online thoughts on collaboration garnered among associates.

SECTION 2

WISDOM GARNERED FROM LISTENING

'GARFOSS'

‘Money equals freedom to exploit’
JOURNEYING ON, IN DEBT TO DIALOGUE

What stirs through the endless echo of a stable in Bethlehem,
both real and as envisioned in committed undying hope?

It lies in facing up to the love of power,
its offspring, usurious exploitation, casino mentality;
that we may journey on in the flow of emergent co-evolution,
and the grace of God, wrestling the deep questions of our existence;
thus moving on from:
war - **to** - peace
ego-systems - **to** - eco-systems
competition - **to** - collaboration
chains of command - **to** - webs of co-operation
blind financial markets - **to** - fair trading networks
controlling hierarchies - **to** - inclusive holarchies
and so, from love of power **to** power of love.

Thus, the power of powerlessness transcends,
awakening the four chambers of the global heart,
our common earth identity, our prior unity,
where ‘not-two is Peace’ held in the wholeness
of all opposites, reaching for Omega.

Incarnation is the path of spirit materialised,
fleshed as potential love, in every form of animation.

Explore that potential in one another, encourage
shared pursuit of the Common Good in dialogue
with all you meet. Shared dignity will lead
from animosity to equality
in birthing the Kin-dom of the Ground of all Being.

From localised daily explorations of the 'Kin[G]dom of God.'

'Owning our nation's spirituality'
THE INTENTION OF THIS GLOBAL OPEN TABLE

The Global Open Table, in welcoming all
is not to serve encultured images
but to question them.

Be nurtured persistently to hold
'All your convictions tentatively', and to
'Throw out all dogma and take it back as poetry,'

While ever challenging and replenishing
'High tolerance for ambiguity'.
Thus pursuing inclusive universal truths.

We seek to set every subject raised
both in universal context and local applications.
Thence diligently enabled to pursue every course
towards the Inclusive Common Good.

'Umuntu ngumuntu ngabantu'
'I am because We are'
African Proverb

Meeting around an imagined open table has persisted for more than 20 years.

‘Seeking a new Gaian Paradigm’
EVOLVING CONSCIOUSNESS - NOW OR NEVER

Current global crises teach us that humanity
must evolve in consciousness,
far beyond what it thinks is intelligent,
far beyond its pride in technology,
far beyond ingrained, encultured egotism.

We need to seek free springs of knowledge
flowing directly from a new Sun Paradigm
with urgent rediscovery of eternal gifts,
history’s great triad, – Faith, Hope and Love –
lived in societal structures of just co-operation.

If these three ways of knowing fire together
as ecology, they’ll boost us out of the orbit of
stupidity and self-centeredness, allowing
humanity to rise to higher consciousness
or fatal harm strikes our fragile planetary soil.

It is our collective responsibility of genuine wisdom,
to advance the evolution of the Common Good
in our very Ground of Being.
Yes, each of us must do the inner work to devolve
into a common resource steps we each can make.

‘Pure interest’ is what we’ll add; replacing encultured
structural interests of extortionate money lending.

Changing gear, not our dress; a vital interest in inclusive
justice
on the road to peace, as our new Sun Paradigm
clearly emphasises and integral perceptions rapidly
evolve.

Open Table talk across the ether, week after week as the search for sanity goes on.

'Healing our traumatised society'
COHESION IN ECOLOGICAL IDENTITY

Gaian and Quantum feedback requires values at once
Intimate [**Self-scape**]
Corporate [**Social-scape**], and
Global [**Earth-scape**], in which our
observations, settings and experiences
permanently oscillate [**Poietic-scape**] to
become emergent in systemic sensibilities.

Thus the call to nurture a psyche the size of the universe
[**Gaian/Quantum identity**],
[**tight-coupling with the earth**], within which
to perceive our ecologically humble,
economically response-able true self.

Such response to the imperative
for inclusive justice
will arrive only with publicly created money,
free of interest, loaned into productive use,
with ensuing assets held in new proportion
to the continuing Common Good, and
with that 'legal person', corporate law,
being held accountable for society
and the protection of fragile planet earth.

Only thus can be reborn a medium of exchange
that works for everyone and protects the earth.

Discussions on countering 'A culture of socially acceptable cheating', the theme of 'A Traumatised Society', F Harrison – and relating the Universal Christ, to incarnation and the potential in each of us to build parts of the Kin[G]dom of God.

'Seeking a new universal Paradigm of Integrity'
PRAYING AND ACTING WHEN WAR RAGES

War brutalizes and we know it.
Most of us are not in direct combat.
But we are assaulted by relentless news stories
trying to hold our attention hostage
while numbing us to human suffering.
The black-and-white narratives,
the moral and political posturing,
polarization and social fragmentation wear on us.
It's difficult to remain open, interested, caring,
or even to know what to do.

We need to create space to deepen our humanity
in the face of the actual war,
exploring the deeper questions
of how to defend the peacefulness
of society and ourselves.
What future do we want to leave behind us?
What do we each want to uphold, honour,
and even in our ageing, still work for?
How can we embody that *now?*
How to develop the spiritual strength to handle
complexity, uncertainty, trouble in these times?

Discussing our understanding of 'Ubuntu' and 'Love of every neighbour', or we will perish.

'Comparing the laws of man and nature'
ALLODIUM REIGNS, IMPOVERISHING GAIA

World news floods with concern for the poor,
yet symbols of vested interest, the rich
are safe behind their exploitative closed door,
unconscious of the extent of their ill pitch.

Profoundly significant words oft fade from use,
when challenging encultured behaviour.
One grotesque, if hidden, form of this abuse
of Gaia's gifted **COMMON WEALTH** all should favour,

lies in a faded word, a deep conceit, '**ALLODIUM**'.
'Estate held in absolute ownership, acknowledging no superior'.
It identifies the few who occupy life's power podium:
beneath which all earth's animation grows ever more inferior.

The poor for whom we feel increased compassion
now include wind and wave, land and ocean,
bird, beast, flora, fauna, all matter macro- and micro-cosmic,
belittled by this major mortal sin, **THEFT OF THE COMMONS**,
the extreme arrogance of legally allowing **ALLODIUM.**

Associates debating the 'Theft of the Commons' as a key structural fault perpetrated by humans.

'Science and Spirituality harmonising our understanding'
BEYOND BOUNDARIES TO MYSTIC BOUNTY

We can no longer entertain evidence,
culturally deemed to be true,
[ceteris paribus: all other things being equal]
in studies with impermeable boundaries.
When reality is unbounded, full of inequalities
in vital rich diversity, vibrant in cosmic Prior Unity.

Brian Cox[1] and Matthew Fox[2] steer us so appealingly,
through and far beyond the solar system,
towards *new* insights into the universe
evolving wherever mind or eye should stray:
leading our consciousness into that
seamless virile realm of Prior Unity.

Tribalism in human specialisms
has validity and value only when
helping to conceive the cosmic integrity
from which life, so abundant, ever flows.
It flows in water, H_2O, simply, profoundly,
into untold abundance created everywhere.

[1]Prof. Brian Cox - astute popular interpretations of Space science
[2]Rev. Matthew Fox - of 'Original Blessing' and studies in Mysticism

Discussions informed by Cox and Fox on Science and Faith.

'Exploring the reaches of Mysticism'
AWESTRUCK & RESPONSIBLE

Awestruck by the incomparable humanity of the astounding Jesus, we realise that if our witness is to be to profound inclusiveness, we need to consciously represent:

A radiant cry of mutual respect, defeating enemies by making them our friends;
maintaining and exercising all these inseparable polarities
to sustain their natural retaining perspective of creative tension
within earth's eternal thrust for life.

Yin AND Yang [*the fundamental paradox of creative polarities*]
Sunny Side AND Shady Side [*root of yin and yang*]
Macrocosm AND Microcosm - Whole AND Parts [*at every level of scale*]
Soul AND Body [*value of this distinction*]
Imagination AND Mind [*the ordinate first is wider than the second*]
Inherent Integrity AND Rich Diversity - Prior Unity AND Nurturing Tribalisms

Inseparable Love of God AND Neighbour as yourself!
Prophetic [*retaining perspective*] AND Pastoral [*attentiveness and care in acts of chaplaincy*]
Prayerful-ness AND Training Exercises [*i.e. developing a 'mind of Christ'*]
Gladness AND Sadness [*pain as a signal not a defeat*]
Danger AND opportunity [*in every crisis or critical turning*]
Global Society AND Local Individual [*Gaian Planet Management in every act*]!
Christ Likeness – Jesus Exemplar [*saviour in that sense*]
Prophet/Pastor [*potential in* all] AND Priest [*interim enabling role of any individual*]

THE BODY IS IN THE SOUL: THE SOUL IS NOT CONFINED WITHIN THE BODY

A composition in early years of the London Global Open Table, itself an extension of the Christian Council for Monetary Justice's theme from 1962.

'In flight towards the Common Good'
A CROW'S PERSPECTIVE

Crows prepare their day atop a tree:
hardly a nest, a point of comprehensive view,
set betwixt the Cosmos, Gaia, the Garden.

Such is its sensitive appraising of
the macro and micro scaled elements
of life born of the strength of spirit and energy
flowing from the Ground of all Being, even
into our very own home and garden below.

This view gifts room to all space and place,
for all incarnate creativity to thrive:
the miniscule and mighty, flesh, soil and plant,
positively investing in their own awakening
to conscious recognition of Prior Unity.

God is the creative impulse in all creation,
Big Bang through Eternity, set for us
in permeable boundaries of all earthly relationships.
Faithful commitment comes ever
with an inherent sensitivity toward three persons.

God as the cosmic creative force of love.
Humans with love as real potential in their incarnation.
Spirit as the love for every, even bothersome, neighbour.
A trinitarian bonding all being for the Common Good.

A doubly wise commandment in triple form,
'Love God and your neighbour as your greater self'.
Note the significance of order in very sharp reversal
of the norm of the ego's self-centred starting point.

Life-blood for all creation is Godly cosmic energy
pulsing evermore diversely through this sacred earth.
Only thus do we love our neighbours, often out of sight;
the Kith and Kin of all animation throughout sacred
Gaia.

The ordinary is the source of that meaning only when
we view the extra creative wonder of a Crow's tree-top
view.

Thus may we be faithful to human purpose in
stewarding,
nurturing, releasing the creative impulse in all life
about us.

Garden communities discuss a persistent lesson from the birds.

'Discussions on how we really are made of stardust'

FORMATION AND REFORMATION OF ENERGY AS MATTER

The spirited phenomena of the cosmic mystery,
is manifest in the Gaian sphere; wherein
the gift of God lies in perpetual incarnation,
energy forming and transforming into matter,
exemplary gifting in the conception of every child,
the formation of a mountain, the raging of the sea;
macro and micro formations of infinite scale.

Ever as spirit/energy becomes matter,
matter ever reverts to energy.
The circulating flow proceeds at various speeds,
each appropriate to the form of animation
or the nature of materialisation we see.
So on every mountain, beside each stream,
recall the eternal life of which you dream.

It is a spread of life journeying the path of
Nature > Nurture > Maturity > Eternity
with given roles and legacies for each in every
aspect of our universal community feeling
for the enlargement of Common Good.
A complex role, captured in a simple word,
Ubuntu: 'I am because We are'.
To change a system, deal with the bottlenecks
'Exploitation by Usury', 'Theft of the Commons',
'Instituionlised Hierarchies' - Greed.

Discussion on 'The nitrogen in our DNA, the calcium in our teeth, the iron in our blood, the carbon in our apple pies were made in the interiors of collapsing stars. We are made of starstuff.' Carl Sagan.

'A path from Celebrities to Actors in building an Inclusive Economy'
TOKYO'S TOKENISM

While euphoria still echoes round the room,
about things viewed in Olympics 2021 by zoom;
'out of this world', 'over the moon', 'Oh my God',
'fantastic', 'unbelievable', 'amazing', 'incredible',
'extra-ordinary', abounding examples of individuals and their teams
expressing the outcome of patient and persistent preparation,
with the encouragement of skills instilled by familial training.

Is this not a glimpse, hint, open aspiration, of evolutionary enterprise,
as seeded at every birth; the wonder enclosed within
that profound term 'incarnation', potentiality available eternal creativity,
seen in every tiny sphere each occupies within the cosmic vastness.
Such spirited energy which has expanded for the supereon since Big Bang.
'Oh my God'. How now to convert such dedication and discovered glory
in our own drive for the Common Good as one
'international human team.'

What mutuality, what enduring training, what end
outcomes?
Yes, unique opportunities to serve and not to count the
cost,
to see the outcome not of individual medals or near
misses
but the true sharing of the Common Good.
What is the use of that marvellous Olympic global
viewing
of personal best or new world records, massive
achievements,
if we do not diligently apply expertise and training to
life ourselves;

to the tasks of structural change ahead, the end of
usury,
the passing on of earth's gifts without possessiveness,
the evolving of co-operation as the basic mode
of not only Olympic aspiration, but that of the salvation
in perpetual evolution of nature's eternal gift,
integral life in its prior unity expressed ever in rich
diversity.
Let's all birth anew each day such euphoria.

Dialogue translating Olympic fervour for structural redesign and application.

'Why Habitat Destruction, Invasive Species, Pollution, Over-Harvesting?'
INTEGRATION SLOWLY DAWNS

Burgeoning accounts of discovering
the reign of integrity throughout creation
emerge in a new cosmic consciousness,
warming to the Sun Paradigm that must replace
the Dark Paradigm in which the mind of humans
has been warped, twisted and bewildered.
Yet eagle-like flights of fancy are soaring in,
winging in a view of integration, sowing hope,
where pessimism has been fast gaining ground.

Integrity is often glimpsed then lost
in our contemporary culture.
When during any human exchange
rare moments come when trust
is clearly felt, most people will reveal
deep aspirations for sanity, justice and peace
to reign over our locality and community.

But every Monday convention reigns again
In facing responsibility to the job at hand.
So we all resume life in the reigning culture,
with its focus on self in local conditions
of comfort and reward, a wage, content
that wider responsibilities are left to others.

Integration of our bodies and brains; integration of our individual lives and corporate lives; integration of nutrition with mental health; and integration of personal wellbeing with societal safety and justice. In all of these aspects of integrity, we wish you rest, new perspective, encouragement, insight, and bravery, to comprehend a new paradigm.

'Why the eye needs a context of long memory'

THE EYE THAT SPIES REALITY

Let's sense and improve our two eyed vision,
one unblinkered, our 'semiotic eye';
the other blinkered, by habitual egotism.
Both aid sight keenly, but confusingly:
integrity perceived only through contextual clarity.

True vision gives life integrity and particularity.
One deep-focussed eye interprets contextually
the content of the other's local zone of witness,
in its unique expression in present time and place
of incarnation, that birthed potential to be 'in Christ'.

THE MEMORY THAT DISTORTS OR FADES

As we all grow older present memories jostle
with persons, time and place bewilderingly.
Weakening memory tries vainly to locate
where vital data is safe but hidden from recall.

Though Laptops are copious aiding discs
the whereabouts of items needed now,
matters of particular urgent pertinence,
where so much information can be kept,
can't straight forwardly be found.
Pen and paper are essential despite AI.

Poems address mysterious reality sufficiently obliquely that we can sense the truth aslant. Through attentive listening the poem becomes an invitation to experience creation's integrity.

SECTION 3

HOLISTIC, IMMERSIVE AND COSMIC

FAITH SPECIFICS

'It is very hard for evil to take hold of the un-consenting soul'

HISTORIC JESUS AND THE UNIVERSAL CHRIST

The one a human example,
the other a title depicting the witness
of any who have made manifest
their living for the Common Good.

'In Christ' defines that way of life more pertinently
than the description of one's faith as Discipleship.
'In Christ' defines our actions, '**Discipleship**' gives
a hint of dependence, rather than our need of
inspiration.

The human **Jesus** points to those who learn and follow,
each in their contemporary settings and terms.
The title **Christ** challenges each new generation to
live out the present interpretation of the wisdom of the
ages.

Human development in harmony with nature is the existential challenge of our time. The goal of this reflection is to foster human development as a Common Good and an integral Ecology, in which the terms 'God' and 'Gaia' reflect the sympathetic mutual discernment of spirituality and science. Compassionate listening and genuine humility will raise our consciousness.

The inspiration offered by Matthew Fox in 'Original Blessing'

CORE OF RELIGION IN THE HEART OF EXPERIENCE

The core of religion lies,
not by dwelling on doctrines that so easily divide,
even within religious traditions,
but in the heart's experience of living.
Embrace the common faith of deep ecumenism,
in essence, Love God in loving every neighbour.
Seek to distil the common principles of all faith searchings,
in all our Gaian planet's varied settings
to show how the different fingers of all faiths
connect unwittingly to God's single hand.

This common origin and goal approach to life,
will inspire us to embrace deep ecumenism,
the manifestation of YAHWEH, the one 'I Am'.
Integral - the jigsaw in which everyone has missing pieces - if only the neighbours in our present picture.
In all true wit and wisdom
integral faith must mean a body of people
not the innate materials providing local symbolic focus.
The jigsaw is an analogy of the entire gamut of family,
community, neighbourhood, town, country, nation,
all meteorological zones, Gaia and, via the sun,
out into the whole of our birthing cosmos.

Distilled from dialogue in a Supported Housing Community.

'Retaining the insights of our nurture'
LEARNT IN MY NURTURE

To speak boldly to evoke, but out of '**tentative conviction**',
never from hardened certainty.

To favour my own conditioning but retain an '**high tolerance for ambiguity**', letting otherness in.

To '**Throw out all dogma to take it back as poetry**',
True mysticism, not managerialism, then lives on.

I learnt also from my blood father that **we share a spirit 'father/mother'**
in the ceaseless creativity of God.

I grasped the simple truth of **mutual servant ministries**
from my mother's un-obtrusive passion
first in sensing, thence in experiencing,
life for others.

One step thence to accepting Jesus as my example in the pilgrim way,
as '"**in Christ" shall all be made alive.**'

No consequent surprise that '**Universe**' and '**God**', for me, are **One**,
matter as energy in many vibrations

For **spirit is matter seen in a stronger light**
God is the union of all opposites.

'Being well adjusted to a very sick society is not a sign of health'
Seek **'Work the soul must have.'**
Know that **'Beauty is in the second glance,
after you have dealt with the prejudice of the first.'**
And that **'Poverty is frustrated potentiality.'**

Written after being asked to tell a 13 year old what I had learnt as a young man - all those years ago!

'Living with mystery not relying on expletives'
LIFE'S FULL FORCE IN A SMALL METAPHOR

Provocative enough to force an 'O My God!'
Evocative enough to shape a purpose in life's meaning
Vocative enough to fashion a life's pattern
for each of us to follow.
Thus our open minds conceive
a new consciousness that contains, companionably,
vast mystery and everyday reality,
hidden behind that simple human metaphor.

As that full force, 'I Am', dawns upon us
we see the whole ever in all parts,
creation flowing as eternal life, finding form
and manifestation in elements, galaxies, animals,
plants, humans and all the endless faces
emerging from and speaking through that
tiny metaphor of one self-emptying 'God',
infusing inherent dignity in all,
deserving our respect and appreciation.

Once expressed as: 'Everything is a holon replicating
the whole'
Now we see how anyone can come to sense God,
starting with humble and simple things,
moving inspirationally on from there.
Meaning in our life is found, in a first step,
ascending to find ourselves materially entire,
as energised-spirit flowing as creative crafting
of the wisdom and benevolence shining
forth in all created and evolving things.

First, love ocean rocks and earth's elements.
Then, trees, plants, animals, birds, humans,
sensing a mysterious symbiotic harmony.
Discover in conscious human awakening
innate beauty and goodness in all creation,
that we can now enjoy divine flow in all nature.
Force of life in that rich metaphor unites everything
in universal attraction and appreciation.
Enlightenment helps questioning minds
acknowledge all nature in that brief metaphor.

Challenging ourselves on using expletives when surprised, shocked, startled, delighted.

'Revisiting the meaning of eternity'
RESURRECTION'S LEGACY

Might not resurrection relate to human lives
as unfolding legacy, thus profoundly to eternity.
God's unceasing creative love flows through all life,
all figments, all livelihoods, all Gaian growth;
a ceaseless source of energy throbbing
between highly energised spirited force
and interim infinite materialisations.

Resurrection feeds the soul,
that it in turn may inspire the body,
giving it identity in voluntary discipleship
to that way toward maturity seen in
the unfading legacy of the humble,
historic profundity of Jesus,
exemplifying consistent life 'in Christ'.

A simple summary of profound mysteries:
UBUNTU - I am because we are.
HUMANISM WITHIN A MYSTERY - behind all faiths.
INCARNATION - cosmic energy in each of us.
CO EVOLUTION - co-creative transformation.
UBIQUITOUS CREATIVE ENERGY.
SACRED LIFE WITHIN A SACRED PLANET.
CONTINENTAL HUMAN TRUSTEESHIP
- for all things under the rainbow.

A discussion on the viability of earth as a home for humanity and the platform for our role in the universe.

'Pondering original meanings of our dogmas'
ARAMAIC SHOWS WHAT TRANSLATED REPETITION MISSES

Ponder the wonders and the woes of words.
Watch patiently your own too ready use, and
your perception of the studied words of others.
Recall that child who innocently called God 'Harold',
as the Lord's Prayer tripped repetitiously,
habitually, from adult tongues, Hallowing the 'Name'.

So let's face the challenge of the conventional Lord's Prayer
in recent scholarly translation from its Aramaic birth.
Debate its unexpected stimulation in translation.
Is it possible that **'Do not cling to me'**
may not have been a rebuke but an invitation
for Mary Magdalen to see her beloved rabbi and friend
from a new perspective?
Could the same invitation apply to us?

THE LORD'S PRAYER TRANSLATED FROM ITS ARAMAIC ORIGINAL

O Birthed Father-Mother of the Cosmos you create all that moves in light.
Focus your light within us - make it useful: as the rays of a beacon show the way.
Create your reign of unity now - through our fiery hearts and willing hands.
Your one desire then acts with ours, as in all light, so in all forms.
Grant what we need each day in bread and insight: subsistence for the call of growing life.
Loose the cords of mistakes binding us, as we release the strands we hold of others' guilt.
Don't let us enter forgetfulness, but free us from un-ripeness.
From you is both all ruling will, the power and the life to do,
the song that beautifies all, from age to age it renews.
Truly - power to these statements - may they be the source
from which all my actions grow.
Sealed in trust and faith. **So be it.**

A discussion on ending dogma by examining the humble, poetic probing that gave it birth.

'Recalling earth citizens from their nationalist pride'
FROM ALIEN TO CITIZEN

As resident aliens immune at once,
to the entire 'KIN', family of earth citizens,
to the **'G'** within, the **Ground of all Being,**
to the '**DOM**inion' of light and energy,
we dis-respect all creative expressions
of the **KIN[G]DOM** of light, of love, of God.

As resident citizens instead, follow,
personally, communally, politically,
the light and word of a universal
Christ-filled '**POLITIC**',
As communal, life-enhancing
Common-God, Common-Wealth,
in synergistic, simultaneous, variety.

As Earth Citizens become no longer aliens,
but aroused by a metabolic mind-shift,
a paradigm change, to hold
in ever flowing creative tension,
a strong love of planetary integrity,
embracing respect for every manifestation
of a universal togetherness in rich diversity.

So, thriving planetary citizenship flourishes
In non-party, singular participation,
in a Christ-energised community, or '**POLITIC**',
boasting co-evolutionary diversity,
that every viewing person respects integrity
flowing as distinctive diversity, heralding on
earth, the **KIN[G]DOM OF GOOD GOD**, no less.

From open table collaborative exchange.

'Discuss enlarging the concept and content of the soul'

SOUL ETERNALLY EMBODIED IN EACH PLACE

'Wherever you stand, be the soul of that place,'
said Rumi, touching a nerve while further exploring
a great key secret behind our human yearning.
'The soul is not in the body, the body is in the soul.'
'My' soul or 'Yours' is an anachronism and conceit,
obscuring the finest focus for the cosmos entire,
the ceaseless creativity we narrowly call, 'God'.

'I AM' is one God, unbelittled by human interpretations,
soul extant in perpetual motion, bestowing free gifts
of vibrant life and love to galaxies, genomes and girls;
to boys, boulders, bedrooms; even to Benidorm.
Such interpretation of soul allows every embodiment
to have boundless potential, always an element of cosmic
integrity flowing on through eternity,
each freely making unique contributions
to and for universal good or ill.

Fear of death can only be conquered on realisation
That, as there is one life in the universe,
and life thrives ever as eternity. Then we can say
'I am in everything, in everybody; I am in all lives;
I am the universe,' Only then comes full faith in
'I AM'
and so, fearlessness.

From a Global Open Table wrestling with the meaning of Soul in relation to our daily lives.

'The composition of our faithful convictions'
CREEDAL ULTIMACY

'I BELIEVE' is at some time heard on every tongue.
But we must all soon recognise it in nature's terms.
Truth can tolerate no ultimate diversity of creeds.
Global peace, harmony, replenishment, even survivability,
Exist ubiquitously as a single creed, manifestly true.

WISDOM can only validly be an inclusive wisdom,
Paralleled in every vestige of a sole Gaian cosmic orb.
Humans all agreeing there is but one most simple wisdom,
Whose profound influence is infinite integrity, displaying
An eternal intensity of beauty in its evolving new creations.

'WE BELIEVE' defines a new Sun Paradigm we must own.
In the discovery of that supreme and terrible mystic beauty
'Being-with', 'co-essence', 'co-appearance', 'co-existence'
Reminding us all that 'a single being' is a contradiction,
No other paradigm, no sovereignty, only '**ALL BEING**'.

Born of a parish meeting discussion in a mood of alarm at world trends and the decline of formal church attendance.

'Intermittent prayer or daily prayerfulness'
A CRITIQUE of 'DAILY PRAYER' for THY KINGDOM COME

The 'Daily Prayer' to God, endorsed by the Archbishops,
seems to imply God 'for us.'
Yet incarnation infers that 'God' is a verb,
not a noun, integrity universally 'with us'.
The 'Prayer initiative', from Ascension to Pentecost,
weighs upon us like a call for recruitment
to the extant divisive church.

Conversely the Jubilee Roadmap of 2012
guides our daily prayerfulness,
our intentions together for the Common Good,
with all the energy, creativity
and bold spirited witness possible for us
in reconciliatory collaboration,
to serve creatively the intimate, corporate and global
complexity of our integrated societal lives.

The Jubilee approach offers roadmaps
and images of co-operation for integrity
in forming the fabric of a recovered society
alive with nature's harmonies.
"Natural Inclusion is Communion of love in life and life
in love."
It sustains the creative tensions between
'God and every neighbour',
'Form and formlessness', 'Space and time',
'Free Energy and Specific Presence',
'Spirit and Matter', and
String Theory in all its 10 dimensions
of 'God's' cosmic formations as the 'Ground of Being'.

As Capitalism fails, we need a roadmap to restore inclusive justice.

‘Prayerfulness as a perspective for each day’
NESTING NOT RESTING TO START EACH DAY

Today, as dawn clouds filtered out the stars,
crows took up their lofted viewing points,
their platforms atop tall trees, to absorb
the morning’s contemplation of the day ahead,
to spot its potential possibilities, or to plan
details of broadly preconceived tasks or pleasures.

Likewise, thoughtful people pause at start of every day
to ensure in contemplation, the natural cosmic context,
beneath the stars, above the previously mundane,
in which to design the way into all specific acts,
dreamt, intended or stumbled on..
We all must face full Context before we start our day.

With a daily garden view before all residents, this community talks often of the lessons learnt from birds

Visit **https://SunParadigm.org** for the new Paradigm we must adopt.

SECTION 4

CRISES OF THE 2020's

RESTRUCTURING

'We must absorb the Big Bang and Gaia themes'
WHAT'S ALL THE NOISE ABOUT?

As we acknowledge Big Bang
our voyage through eternity begins.
Accepting that single origin of all energy,
we can sense each animation as an original
in inter-dependence with all earth's kith and kin.

There are known and unknown details of reality.
We are humbled by Big Bang's burst into life,
allowing us a privilege, our sense of stewardship
of a tiny vital passage, just one human lifetime,
within spirit/energy's ever-creative, flow.

This allows us to reimagine, redesign life on earth,
noting James Lovelock's passing in July 22 at 103;
a bold, perceptive pioneer of 'Gaian' explanation
of all above as channelled through the sun,
locating humanity's kith and kin in sacred setting.

A discussion of Thomas Berry's 'The universe is the primary revelation of the divine, the primary scripture, the primary locus of divine-human communication.'

'Accelerating the expansion of consciousness'
SHOT IN THE DARKNESS OF OUR BLINKERED PARADIGM

Its horror reverberates through all humanity.
Another senseless mass murder rattles all self-satisfaction.
Ukraine, Texas, Mass Migration of the fearful,
Pandemic alarms,
make unarguably clear that no one can be fully human,
until all are allowed their naturally birthed, stable dignity.

The crossroads 'twixt common good and remorseless ill,
must be acknowledged and our clear choice made.
The universe, feels hostile, though its creation
is a freely offered gift of spirited energy
versed in materialised inclusive justice.

Once more the last chance cry is to be heard.
Abolish exploitation inherent in three structural foundations:
Usurious money system, exponentially destructive.
Theft of the Commons, legal under the conceit of Allodium.
And Patriarchal institutions of vested interests.

Collaborative exchanges on motives behind any false sense of security. Visit https://SunParadigm.org - a Paradigm we must adopt.

‘Expanding awareness must breed decisive action’
WINNING OR FAILING BY TURNING A BLIND EYE?

Darkness is natural in the daily round,
the Yin and Yang of all creation.
But now the scale and spread of global drought
Is a brown shadow and foreboding of creeping rout
of adequate fertility and food availability for
animated communities across the earth entire.

A positive rising SUN PARADIGM
must soon extend our consciousness
affirming Gaian integrity for all our planet’s life,
inspiring inclusive action for the Common Good.

Present negativity of the DARK PARADIGM
Tempts us inevitably to flee
by choosing protestation before pertinent proposals,
that all can coordinate by a persuasive critical mass.
Or by complaining loudly and not acting humbly
each in our own way.

Flourishing community exchanges occurring randomly awaiting decisive action.

'Facing different challenges in each nation'
LET'S FACE IT, BRIDGE IT, SURVIVE

The challenge every faithful one must face.
Am I pursuing a private salvific project
or feeling the force of Nature's free nudging
by God's endless, exhilarating creativity?
Environmental pressure is simply persistent,
adaptive evolution, acting on spirited impulse.

'A Bridge Too Far', that wishful, pragmatic,
unprincipled excuse, tempts us too easily.
But in the quanta reality now dawning on us all,
nature requires we reach that distant crossing,
passing over from narcissistic competition
to celebrate in communal collaboration.

Thus, we still can provide for all
by commitment to the Common Good,
accommodation in a global family, claiming
indiscriminate inclusive justice and
substituting endless war by peace.
We can only face this communally.

Emerging from dialogue on the strength of our community.

'Our legacy of lives, not bank accounts'
LEAVE A LEAF FROM YOUR LIFE AS LEGACY

African violets bear potential legacy in every leaf,
new plants emerging from watered sun-catching soil.
Link this rare fact to 'The Sun is the Lord of Life',
a poem by happily named Iris Tree of mid 1900s.

They boldly amplify the imagery of language
during perplexing times of change or loss.
For Libertarians, freedom of speech concerns
the autonomy of atomized individualism.

But Democrats believe essentially in community,
defining how individuals relate in fellowship
through patterns of self-government,
determined by mutuality and seeking of the Common Good.

Fellow residents, incarnate beings all,
have let God-given potential evolve to become their legacy
through lives of loving service, exemplified by Jesus in his
enduring inspiration of every life enthused by God.

Discussion in a Supported Housing Community on the human legacy of each of us.

‘Groups continuing to grapple with the concept of Gaia’
A VISION TO INCLUDE US ALL

Our vision and image of God is holistic, immersive,
a supernatural force birthing our best selves into being
from a scale beyond cumulus clouds whose gilt edges
reach out to God’s glory in crystal skies on sunlit days,
the setting in which we all can comprehend God’s gifts
in all life’s infinite variety, even yours and mine.

Gandhi said, had he only the Sermon on the Mount
as he interpretated it, he’d say, ‘I am a Christian.’
for therein a communal spirit pervades all faiths.
Islam is akin to Judaism on inclusive simplicity,
one cries ‘mend the world’, another ‘morality is love’.
We, and all the universe are not separate entities,
but ‘one functioning whole’, a Zen precept.

In the face of dire need for extensive re-structuring
of societal modes of activity, fear is that to do nothing
would negate the moral core in so many faith forms.
So ask. Would my small action prod others to act too?
Does that even matter, if to stand with the forgotten
is the right thing always to do?

Our dilemma is people everywhere are dutifully
obedient to
Corporate dictates even in face of poverty, starvation,
stupidity, cruelty,
rivalry, even war. A relatively static culture
lets exploitation flourish, ours too.
Return to the first verse to recapture the prime vision
of life on planet earth, God's Gaia.

Gathering themes in widening dialogue on the web of earth - Gaia.

'An essential transition through the sun'
DISASTER DIVERTED BY THE SUN

The sheer proliferation of disastrous trends
leads few to glimpsing a dawning light as
our dependence deepens on the sun's channelling
of cosmic energy through its mystic present passage
into infinite creativity's eternal spiritual supply.

So blazing hot, so winter cool,
so clouded over or as naked heat,
glimpsed or blanketed, it's creative conception
still endlessly births infinite forms of life.
So why have human aspirations to define it,
and comprehend their God and Gaian identity,
taken so long to define and understand despite
the reality of complete integrity in cosmic,
galactic, sun energised, localised aspects
of the all-embracing variety inconceivably in us.

Could it be - ask yourself frankly, then respond -
why have the encultured Theft of the Commons,
exploitative Usurious Money and Patriarchal
Institutions
combined to obliterate all sense of the other
in ourselves, despite creation's pure Integrity?
CODA

Put on the spot! 'What's the basic common issue for humanity today?', we were given ten minutes of the questioner's dedicated time.

'The urgency of rallying a critical mass for structural change'
ALL HANDS ON DECK

All hands on deck before we sink!
Join the common struggle
to save this spaceship earth,
a precious environment,
lovingly conceived as gift,
catalysing earth's all-inclusive
ecological and sociological economy.

For *'No one can be fully human,*
until all are fully human.'
we need to *'live simply,*
that others may simply live.'
In the SUN POWER of spirited mutuality,
as inspirationally materialised
by direct solar energy, Sun's
gifted inherent power we all can use.

The ever Open Global Table encourages collaboration
in teams enthused by solar energy
and new consciousness of Gaian
perceptions of our true nature.

Seeking in neighbourly dialogue a common mind on faith and purpose for humanity in whatever terms they are sought.

'Crisis: sensing danger or seizing the opportunity'
NOW OR NEVER

We are here
on the threshold, the dawn,
of reclaiming our global consciousness,
the restoration of the wisdom of enduring ages.

Now, beyond our nurturing tribal loyalties,
we discern our maturing inclusiveness,
as awareness of how to save the planet
by capturing a cosmic paradigm or law,
simple and profound, offering transformation.

Ponder the deep mystery of Prior Unity,
original, abiding, inherent coherence
born of the cosmos through our sun's energy,
a paradigm of this integral and sacred universe
enabling each one of us from birth to express
our stewarding role in vibrant inter-being.

Let that sense of inter-being define
our monetary system,
the rent we pay for a place on earth,
freedom from patriarchal hierarchies,
thus repaving a moral, ethical, joyful
pilgrim path to Prior Unity stretching out ahead.

From Global OpenTable exchanges about replacing the mindset of egotism as encultured over centuries by expansive ecological awareness.

'Exploring key structural barriers to inclusive justice'
THREE AND THREE FOR SANITY

Climate change is a range of symptoms
needing many urgent **PALLIATIVE** actions; always
within a vital comprehensive structural **CURATIVE.**

But, alas, western governance is gripped by
three exploitive encultured structures,
which must urgently be tackled head on.

USURY, THEFT OF THE COMMONS,
and the institutional rigidity of
POWER-OVER OTHERS, thwarting
COOPERATIVE SHARING
of appropriate skills and tasks.

Our **INTIMATE, SOCIETAL, AND GLOBAL**
SENSIBILITIES
must engage in synchronistic action
at every stage,
if Gaian global integrity is our aim.

Discussion on the core thrust of the Global Open Table network - 3 geared purpose re 3 structural issues that the world community must face and rectify.

'Acting together for the Common Good'
MAKING A DIFFERENCE

Through our own creative actions
we can end dependency on 'The Lord,'
or any institutionalised authority,
obscuring the true dignity of all.

Let us exemplify in our own lives
the creative restoration of nature's one family,
recognise and activate the interaction of

the intimate, corporate and global impacts
of each of our daily actions if judged and
then measured by the 'Common Good':

There is inevitable inter-dependent inclusiveness
of all animated kith and kin in Gaia's planetary life,
if the 'Ground of all Being' is our sense of God.

Help each other to believe in our own
significance in daily positive creativity,
however miniscule each impact may seem to be.

Beyond our naked eyes, each is by nature a universalist,
vitally part of all miniscule particles and giant galaxies.
We must now face-down myopic partisan politics.
deadening the pure purpose of our lives.

From online exchanges at the launch of the 'MAP of CO-CREATORS.'

'Revisiting the Charter of Compassion'
In the CHARTER OF COMPASSION
at the launch of the 'MAP OF CO-CREATORS'
by The Charter of Compassion

This is not a wall to you
it is a call to accept differences
to stand proud to feel safe
and to spread unconditional love.

This is a welcome to every person,
today and always to reject divisions,
to speak your mind,
to be safe outside and in.

Follow this pathway, to awareness,
to acceptance, to compassion.

It is a mission of perverse persistence,
as Adrienne Rich expressed it;
'My heart is moved by all I cannot save,
so much has been destroyed
I have to cast my lot with those
who age by age, perversely,
with no extraordinary power,
Reconstitute the Earth.'

From widespread online exchanges at the launch of the MAP of CO-CREATORS.

FROM THE COMPILER

In my university days I heard *'ceteris paribus'* so many times as, at my tutor JAT Robinson's suggestion, I attended lectures in disciplines other than of my own of Theology. That phrase translated, *'All other things being equal'*, settled in my mind as the root of a profound western human conceit born of rampant encultured narcissism. It served both my studies and subsequent evolving vocation - not least on the 9 month 'Sloan Programme for Potential Corporate Leaders', at the London Business School; an experience that led to my subsequent reflections - **'Personal Aspirations and Corporate Arrogance'** (unpublished).

On my 50th birthday, 42 years ago, a friend wrote 'If you are a poet at 21, you're 21. If you're a poet at 50, you're a poet!'. So, I decided to recover that youthful habit, since neglected, and explore an amateur word - smith's bold search for the intrinsic value in the fullness of creation. I was nurtured in the perception of God as the 'Ground of all Being' and thus to perceive the Kin[G]dom of God as a universal expression of gifted life throughout creation.

Listening to the human life around one, it is surprising how frequently and widely one hears the sudden utterance of 'Good God' or 'Oh my God' or 'Jesus Christ' as a cry of surprise or bewilderment. It seems to represent a conscious or unconscious call or reminder of an ultimate faithful energy guiding us through to the wisdom of the spheres. Wisdom when you need it; 'God' in creation, translated as Integral Life, helping us to make sense of everything with the world's most comprehensive philosophies interpreting the eternal flow of 'energy - into matter - into energy'.

A culture of unrestrained markets has led to a global crisis. Humanity now faces an extensional threat as the result of global dominance by corporations whose ultimate goal is at odds with human flourishing. An egotism that little understands that 'the soul is not in the body, the body is in the soul.' Corporate and Authoritarian dominance is driving human civilisation towards a precipice not far ahead.

When my father died more than 40 years ago, I found his life-guiding mantra atop his neat arrangement of key papers. *'NOTHING IS IMPOSSIBLE FOR THE*

MOST ORDINARY OF US IF ONE DOES NOT MIND WHO GETS THE CREDIT.' In recognition of that pithy summary, I have pursued a longing to face up to the strong river now flooding towards hell on earth, the unchecked flow of our exploitive 'Usurious Monetary System', the ingrained 'Theft of the Commons', and the 'Institutionalised Patriarchal Hierarchies of Control.' These human conceits are interactively fuelling exponential exploitation in so many aspects of our daily lives throughout 'Gaia', 'Mother Earth', our integral living planet.

To that end I have experimented in the stimulation of each day's deliberate or random inflow of words to jot down phrases that are as it were being gifted by GARFOSS to the all-earth inclusive Gaian Kin[G]dom of eternally flowing life. Thus **'The Voice of Listening'** as title to some of my jottings, which are described as finding profound faith in the dignity of mutually attentive dialogue.

The exceptional life and witness of Jesus combined his historic reality with the rich metaphorical universal interpretations, such as Saint Paul discerned. Together they offer to each of us the recognition that we are each and all potentially incarnations as Kin[G]dom dwellers, and even builders.

How does **Gaia**, namely earth's integrity or inclusive kin-ship of all sun-generated fauna and flora, rock and ocean, let wisdom flow freely through our exploratory faithfulness, despite our culturally engendered egotism. Several keywords inform this book's ponderings and jottings.

Jesus - a human of his era, realised his Incarnate potential, his ability to be 'in Christ' and an interpreter and enduring example of the promise and potential inherent in each of us as Kin[G]dom builders. We too have the potential to be 'in Christ', exemplified by Jesus, as persistent incarnation of life and spirit, gifted at birth, even in a stable, as potential with the prospect of evolving materially into service of the Common Good.

Author - deriving from the Latin 'Auctos' and translating as 'Allowing to grow'. When writing or discussing we plant beliefs that might blossom in others in their own context into the just structures of the world. In these times we need new societal structures conceived in a new paradigm sourced in God's free gift of nature as the home of universal inclusive justice, the source of peace.

Religion has provenance in binding all in one, all law, all ligaments. It is a universal state of integrity, not a patchwork of institutional denominational rivalries, valuable as they are in our nurture but less so in genuine maturity, concentrating on people and largely ignoring the structures, so deeply encultured that they are hardly questioned.

Wisdom often flows from even the most unexpected rumblings or close studies. One perceptive wit observed that 'in the public swimming pool the greatest noise comes from the shallow end' as he pleaded for specialists to permeate the boundaries of their disciplines in order to make their insights, when woven together with findings of other disciplines and research, available to all.

Education or schooling? - is a fundamental issue; the first is the respecting of the unique form of potential in every pupil; the second is about cultural impositions formed with little respect for evolution's never ceasing flow.

Go well in contemplation of these probings into sanity.

Peter Challen

ALSO FROM RED BALLOON PUBLISHING

Most Christians know the Protestant Reformation began when Martin Luther nailed 95 'theses' to the church door in Wittenberg, Germany. Whilst these were intended to provoke theological debate, they never managed to deconstruct the church power institution, but bitterly divided it. Had Luther instead emphasised the true nature of God in his theses, the outcome might have been different. Desiring a godly reformation for the church of today, the authors present 96 statements about the three persons of the Trinity, and how each relates to humanity. They argue that God is loving and kind, despite every intimation to the contrary.

In a world awash with deceit and confusion, the authors believe it is vital that believers see God through the lens of kindness, and reject every theological theory that could make us feel hesitant to embrace Him as a dear Father.

Available on Amazon: Nailed: Reclaiming the Gospel

Visit the website: https://tinyurl.com/5yjdyxjp

Printed in Great Britain
by Amazon

22177449R00069